eyewonder

Dinosaurs

THIRD EDITION
Senior Editor Rupa Rao
Project Art Editor Noopur Dalal
Illustrator Aparajita Sen
Picture Researcher Ridhima Sikka
Deputy Manager, Picture Research Virien Chopra
Deputy Managing Editor Sreshtha Bhattacharya
Managing Editor Kingshuk Ghoshal
Managing Art Editors Govind Mittal, Anna Hall
Pre-production Image Editor Mohd Rizwan
Production Editor Vishal Bhatia
Production Controller Joss Moore
Project Jacket Designer Vidushi Chaudhry
DK Delhi Creative Head Malavika Talukder
Associate Publisher Gemma Farr
Art Director Mabel Chan

Consultant Derek Harvey
Factchecker Steve Hoffman

FIRST EDITION
Written and edited by Sarah Walker and Samantha Gray
Designed by Janet Allis
Publishing Manager Mary Ling
Managing Art Editor Rachel Foster
Picture Researcher Jo Haddon
Consultant David Lambert

This edition published in 2025
First published in Great Britain in 2001 by
Dorling Kindersley Limited
20 Vauxhall Bridge Road,
London, SW1V 2SA

The authorised representative in the EEA is
Dorling Kindersley Verlag GmbH. Arnulfstr. 124,
80636 Munich, Germany

Copyright © 2001, 2013, 2025 Dorling Kindersley Limited
A Penguin Random House Company
10 9 8 7 6 5 4 3 2 1
001–348662–Sep/2025

A CIP catalogue record for this book
is available from the British Library.
ISBN: 978-0-2417-3226-7

Printed and bound in China

www.dk.com

MIX
Paper | Supporting
responsible forestry
FSC™ C018179

This book was made with Forest
Stewardship Council™ certified
paper – one small step in DK's
commitment to a sustainable future.
Learn more at www.dk.com/uk/
information/sustainability

Contents

4–5
What is a dinosaur?

6–7
Bony frames

8–9
Dinosaur groups

10–11
Dino worlds

12–13
Mighty giants

14–15
On the move

16–17
Plant-eaters

18–19
Eating meat

20–21
Herd life

22–23
Attack tactics

24–25
Staying safe

26–27
Super senses

28–29
Making a family

30–31
Nests and nurseries

32–33
Taking off

34–35
Inside a dinosaur

36–37
Dinosaur neighbours

38–39
End of the dinosaurs

40–41
All about fossils

42–43
Digging up dinosaurs

44–45
Building dinosaurs

46–47
Facts match

48–49
Where are my eggs?

50–51
Dig that bone

52–53
Dinosaur danger

54–55
Glossary and Animal alphabet

56
Index and Acknowledgments

What is a dinosaur?

Dinosaurs are the most famous prehistoric creatures. But behind the awesome pictures and action movies are real animals that lived in the distant past, and real science that helps us understand them.

Dinosaur skin was covered with scales or feathers.

Carnotaurus, a meat-eating dinosaur

Teeth set in deep sockets, like those of crocodiles

Limbs with flexible joints

 **WALKING UPRIGHT**

The legs of dinosaurs were connected with their shoulder and hip bones further underneath the body – not from the side like lizards and crocodiles.

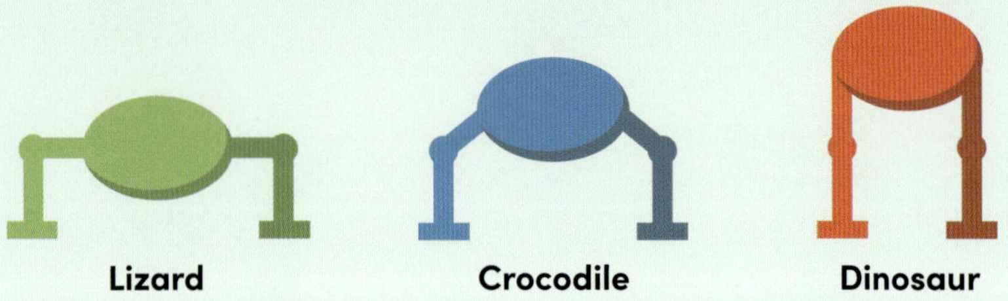

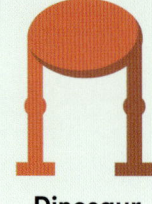

Lizard   Crocodile   Dinosaur

The tail was typically held high for balance.

Dinosaur features

The fossil skeletons of dinosaurs tell us that they were reptiles that had the hard scaly skin of lizards living today. Crocodiles are their nearest living reptile relatives, but dinosaurs had more upright legs that made them more agile.

Fast facts

About 700 kinds of dinosaurs are known from fossils. But more lived that we don't know about.

All dinosaurs went extinct 66 million years ago, except for one group that evolved into feathered birds.

This means that the birds alive today are really living, breathing dinosaurs!

Not a dinosaur

Some well-known prehistoric reptiles were not dinosaurs, but lived alongside them. Flying pterosaurs ruled the skies, while marine reptiles, such as ichthyosaurs, prowled the seas.

Pterosaurs

Ichthyosaurs

BONY PLATES

Some dinosaurs had extra bones that worked like armour. *Stegosaurus* had a double row of 17 bony plates attached to its back, from neck to tail. The plates may have protected it from attackers, or they might have been used for display.

Stegosaurus skeleton

A chain of bones

The backbone stretches from the skull to the tip of the tail. It is made up of lots of smaller bones interlocked together.

Diplodocus had more than 100 bones on its back.

Bony frames

Dinosaurs bodies were supported by a skeleton – just like today's vertebrates (animals with backbones). Most of what we know about dinosaurs comes from studying the fossilized bones of dinosaurs.

Diplodocus

Feather markings

Built for flight

Bird-like dinosaurs, such as *Archaeopteryx*, had hollow bones and flight feathers.

Back legs

Most of a dinosaur's weight was supported by the back legs, so these were usually bigger than the front ones – even in dinosaurs that walked on all fours.

Archaeopteryx fossil

In some dinosaurs, the tail could help balance the body weight.

Dinosaurs walked on their toes.

Two-legged pachycephalosaur

Four-legged ceratopsian

Lizard-hipped dinosaurs

Saurischians were lizard-hipped dinosaurs. Their hip bones were like those of the earlier lizard-like ancestors of all dinosaurs.

Herrerasaurus, an early saurischian

Theropods

Tyrannosaurus rex

The main meat-eaters of the dino world walked upright on two legs. They had small arms and a big head.

Sauropods

Plant-eating sauropods had a long neck, a long tail, and huge legs.

Argentinosaurus

Dinosaur groups

Scientists classify dinosaurs into different groups, just like other animals. The dinosaurs in each group evolved from the same ancestor and had certain features in common.

 HIP SHAPES

The hip bone, or pelvis, of an animal is where its hind legs connect with its body. In lizard-hipped dinosaurs and most other reptiles, part of the hip called the pubis points forwards. In bird-hipped dinosaurs, it points backwards.

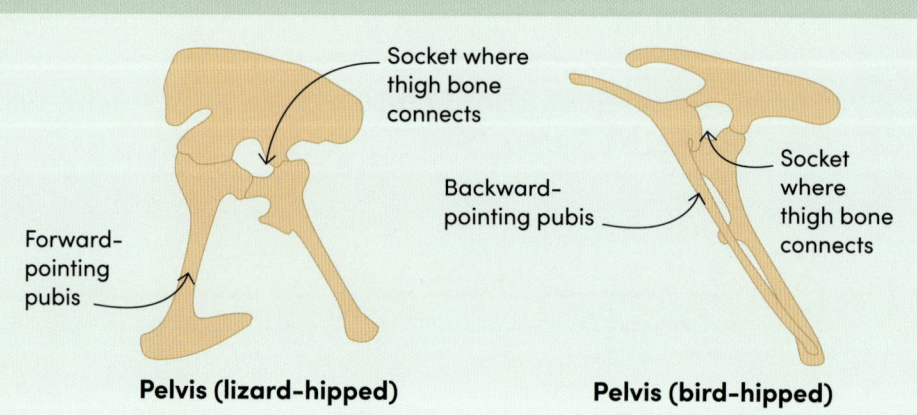

Socket where thigh bone connects

Forward-pointing pubis

Backward-pointing pubis

Socket where thigh bone connects

Pelvis (lizard-hipped)

Pelvis (bird-hipped)

Ankylosaurs

Armoured skin gave all ankylosaurs good defence against the meat-eating theropods.

Ankylosaurus

Stegosaurs

Plates running down the back of a stegosaur might have been used for display as well as defence.

Stegosaurus

Bird-hipped dinosaurs

Ornithischians were bird-hipped dinosaurs that were mainly plant-eaters. They get their name because they had bird-like hip bones, even though they were not directly related to birds.

Heterodontosaurus

Iguanodon

The thick skulls of pachycephalosaurs were probably used to head-butt rivals or meat-eaters.

Triceratops

Standing upright helped ornithopods reach high vegetation, but many also walked on all fours.

Ceratopsians used their head horns to charge at rivals or attack predators, as rhinoceroses do today.

Pachycephalosaurus

Ornithopods   ## Pachycephalosaurs   ## Ceratopsians

Dino worlds

Dinosaurs lived through three periods of Earth's past – Triassic, Jurassic, and Cretaceous. These were times when the world's map, and its climates and habitats, were different from those of today.

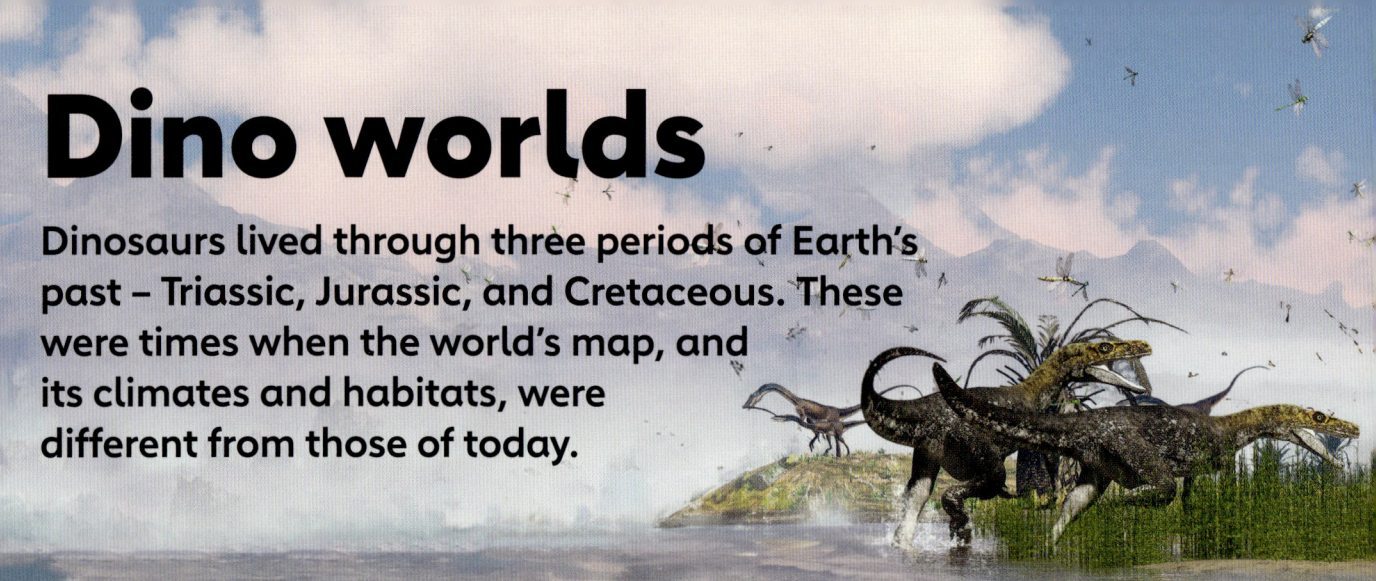

Triassic World

Early dinosaurs were mostly small, such as upright *Coelophysis*, and shared the world's one big, mostly dry continent – Pangaea – with giant crocodile ancestors and the first flying pterosaurs.

201–145 million years ago

Jurassic World

Splitting continents created longer coastlines, more mountains, and greater rainfall. Dinosaurs, including giant long-necked sauropods, lived alongside the first small furry mammals.

145–66 million years ago

Cretaceous World

The greatest variety of dinosaurs appeared with the first flowers and grasses. *Tyrannosaurus rex* (*T rex*) was the most famous predator on Earth. The continents looked more like the ones we know today.

Mighty giants

Some early dinosaurs were no bigger than an adult human, but during their reign they evolved into the biggest animals that ever walked our planet.

👁 BIG AND SMALL

The biggest dinosaurs were long-necked sauropods, with heads higher than a five-story building. The smallest were crow-sized gliders, some of which also learnt to fly.

- 🟨 *Mamenchisaurus*
- ⬛ Adult human
- 🟧 Microraptor

Why so big?
Being the biggest dinosaurs had its benefits – giants could ward off predators and bully other plant-eaters in getting more food. Their big bodies were also better at staying warm and active.

The long neck made it easy for this tall plant-eater to browse on leaves at the treetops.

Mamenchisaurus, a sauropod

Mamenchisaurus's neck was up to 15 m (49 ft) long.

Microraptor

Yangchuanosaurus was an 11-m (35-ft) long theropod that preyed on *Mamenchisaurus.*

Yangchuanosaurus

Tiny flier
The smallest dinosaurs could live on trees. Some of these evolved into the first birds – with arms becoming wings for gliding and flapping.

On the move

All dinosaurs had strong legs with flexible joints for walking on land, but a few evolved wings that helped them take to the air.

On tippy toes

Unlike flat-footed humans, dinosaurs walked on their toes – like birds do – with their bouncy ankles raised high from the ground.

Dinosaurs that walked on their hind legs had more flexible joints.

Struthiomimus, **a theropod**

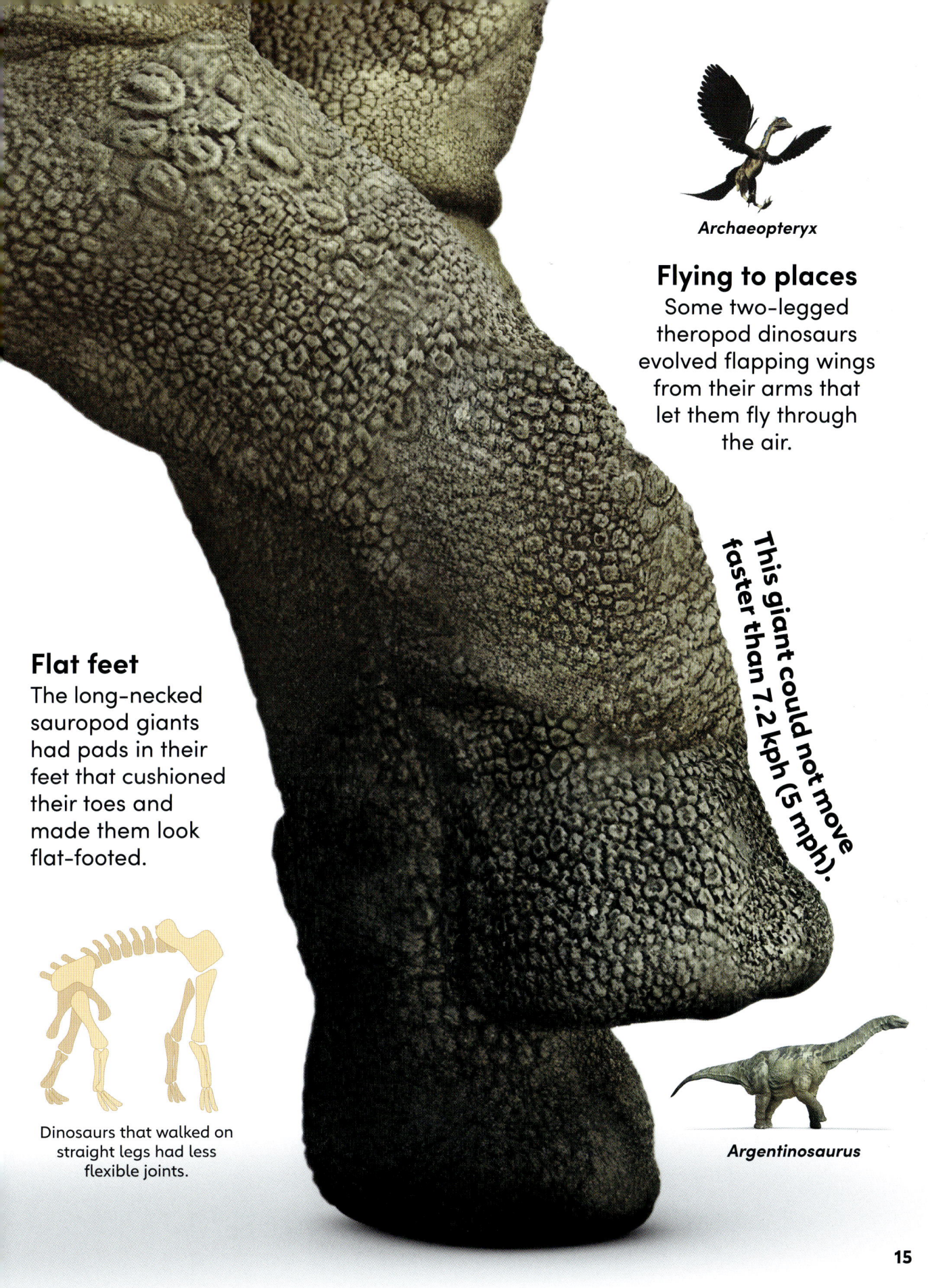

Archaeopteryx

Flying to places
Some two-legged theropod dinosaurs evolved flapping wings from their arms that let them fly through the air.

Flat feet
The long-necked sauropod giants had pads in their feet that cushioned their toes and made them look flat-footed.

Dinosaurs that walked on straight legs had less flexible joints.

This giant could not move faster than 7.2 kph (5 mph).

Argentinosaurus

Plant-eaters

Most kinds of dinosaurs ate plants. Their diet ranged from the leaves of prehistoric ferns to those of ginkgo and conifer trees.

The neck was up to 9 m (30 ft) long.

Ground grazer

An ankylosaur called *Edmontonia* walked with its head close to the ground, so it could only munch on low plants, including ferns and short trees.

Spikes protected this plant-eater from meat-eating dinosaurs.

Tearing teeth

Long-necked dinosaurs such as *Diplodocus* had teeth like pencils. They could pull leaves from tall trees like a garden rake.

Pencil-shaped teeth grew close together.

Duck-billed

Hypacrosaurus and its relatives were called hadrosaurs (a type of ornithopod). This hadrosaur had a mouth shaped like a duck's bill. It contained hundreds of tiny teeth to grind up plants as the animal chewed.

Rows of strong teeth

Brachiosaurus ate 400 kg (880 lb) of plants every day.

Eating tall

The biggest sauropod dinosaurs had long necks to reach leaves of the tallest trees. *Brachiosaurus* also had longer front legs than back legs, and its head could reach twice the height of a giraffe.

Spiny sail was up to 2 m (7 ft) tall.

Eating meat

Dinosaurs that hunted other animals and fed on meat evolved to become some of the largest predators that ever lived. Most of the theropod dinosaurs were meat-eaters.

Fishy food

Spinosaurus was a theropod with long crocodile-like jaws armed with sharp, conical teeth. Scientists think it ate fish.

Herrerasaurus ran on two legs.

Early hunters

The first dinosaurs were meat-eaters. Nimble *Herrerasaurus* probably used its sharp-clawed hands to grapple with prey.

Spinosaurus was one of the largest predators ever on land.

Most clues about dinosaur eating habits come from their fossilized skulls. Meat-eaters had stabbing teeth with cutting blades for tearing through skin and flesh, while powerful jaws could deliver a killing bite.

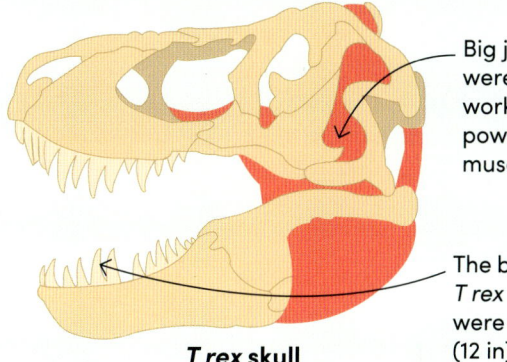

Big jaws were worked by powerful muscles.

The biggest *T rex* teeth were 30 cm (12 in) long.

***T rex* skull**

T rex had a record-breaking bite force – more than twice as strong than that of a living saltwater crocodile.

Powerful predator
T rex had the strength to tackle giant plant-eaters, such as the horned *Triceratops*.

Drawn together

Modern reptiles do not hunt in groups like wolves and lions, so many dinosaurs probably hunted alone too – only coming together to scavenge over carcasses.

A trio of *Austroraptor* feast on the carcass of a dead dinosaur.

Fossils of a herd of Triceratops were found in Wyoming, USA.

Herd life

We know that some dinosaurs lived in groups because lots of their fossils are sometimes found in the same place. It is possible they may have all died together at the same time.

Some fossilized trackways show the footprints of more than one dinosaur. It can often be difficult to identify if these were made by groups moving together, or by separate animals walking over the same place at different times.

Safe together

Dinosaurs were less likely to be targeted in groups. *Triceratops* adults may have surrounded their babies so an attacking *T rex* faced horns from every angle.

Velociraptor had a massive claw on each foot to pierce thick skin.

Clawed hands and feet

Some theropods may have used clawed hands to slash at prey, but the claws on their bigger, stronger hind legs were better weapons.

Attack tactics

Two-legged meat-eaters called theropods had sharp teeth and claws for attacking their prey. They needed brute strength too because sometimes they were facing bigger plant-eaters.

Bite and slice

Allosaurus were large theropods, and might have lunged at big prey, such as *Stegosaurus*, over and over again so their target died of its wounds or exhaustion.

KILLING BITES

T rex was one of the biggest and strongest of the meat-eating theropods. Scientists have studied its skull to work out that its bone-crushing bite was stronger than that of a great white shark.

T rex

Great white shark

Meat-eaters had teeth with serrated edges to cut through flesh.

Fast facts

The biggest theropods with the strongest bites appeared towards the end of the dinosaurs' reign in the Cretaceous Period.

Spinosaurus is the longest theropod discovered so far – up to 14 m (46 ft) from nose to tail tip.

Group attack

A few fossils of meat-eaters, such as *Allosaurus*, have been found grouped together. This shows that some of these dinosaurs may also have hunted in packs to bring down prey.

An *Allosaurus* pack attacks a *Diplodocus*, a sauropod.

Saltasaurus,
a sauropod

Saltasaurus
weighed up
to 2 tonnes.

Quilmesaurus,
a theropod

In plain sight

Psittacosaurus was among the
dinosaurs that could have relied on
the forest cover to stay hidden. Its
skin might have helped it to blend
in among vegetation.

Staying safe

In a world with dangerous meat-
eating dinosaurs, plant-eaters
had ways to protect themselves.
Some probably relied on hiding or
running away, but others used their
size to ward off hunters, or horns or
tails to fight back.

Size and numbers

Giant dinosaurs were often targets for smaller predators, but when they herded together, their sizes and numbers saved many in the herd.

Big plant-eaters might have used their long tails like a whip to try and keep predators away.

Body armour

Stegouros had bony plates called scutes in the skin – just like crocodiles. These scutes worked as a protective armour.

Stegouros, an ankylosaur

Fast facts

Pachycephalosaurus had a thick bony skull it could use to head-butt other dinosaurs.

The tail club of the ankylosaur called *Ankylosaurus* was large enough for an adult human to sit on.

Ankylosaurus tail

Helmet heads

Ceratopsians (horned dinosaurs) such as *Einiosaurus* had protective head armour, including bony frills that might also have been used for displays.

Tail weapons

A heavy tail was a good way to swing weapons. *Ankylosaurus* had a heavy club at the end of its tail, while *Kentrosaurus* had spikes on its tail to fend off attackers.

Tail of *Kentrosaurus*, a stegosaur

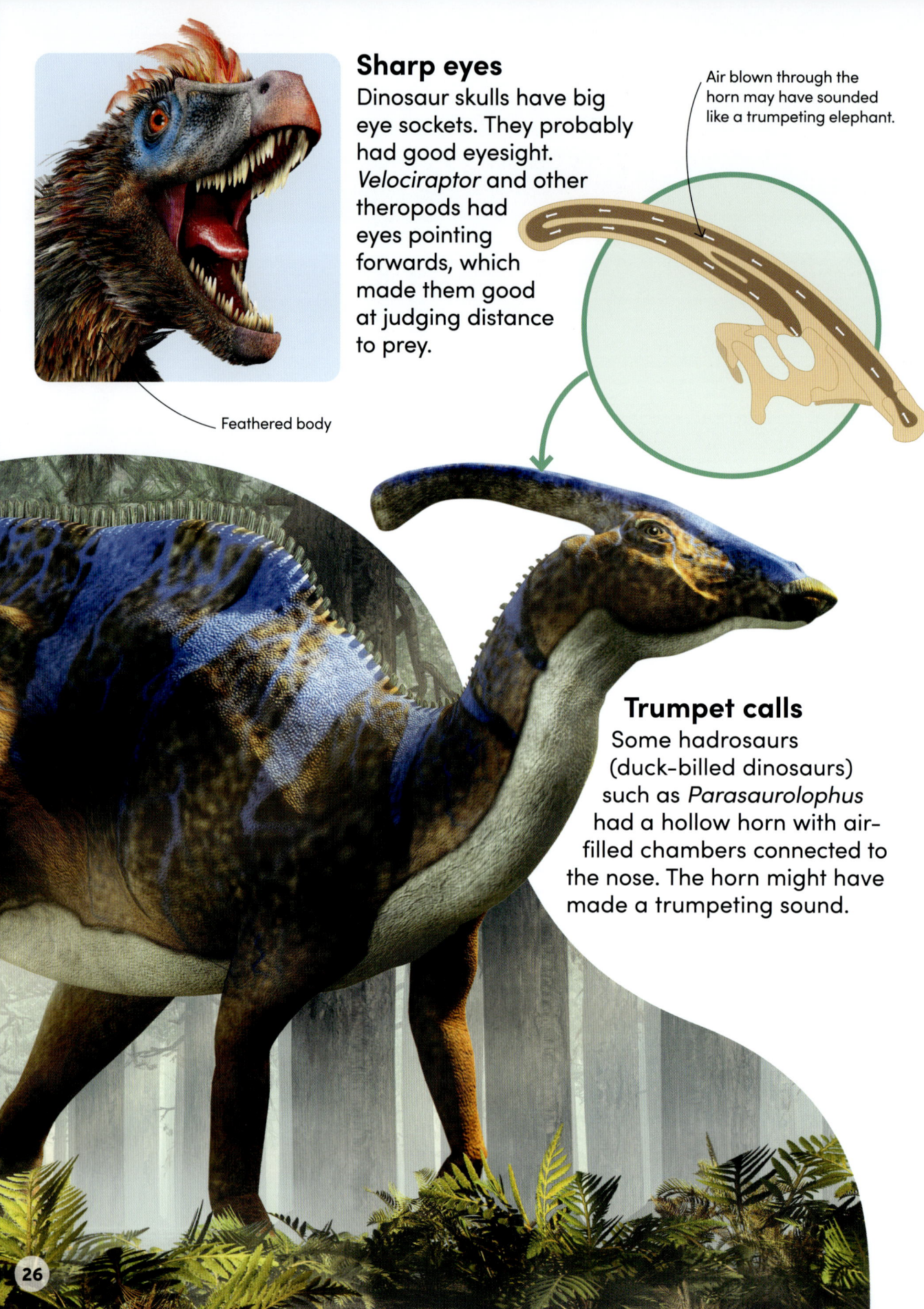

Sharp eyes

Dinosaur skulls have big eye sockets. They probably had good eyesight. *Velociraptor* and other theropods had eyes pointing forwards, which made them good at judging distance to prey.

Feathered body

Air blown through the horn may have sounded like a trumpeting elephant.

Trumpet calls

Some hadrosaurs (duck-billed dinosaurs) such as *Parasaurolophus* had a hollow horn with air-filled chambers connected to the nose. The horn might have made a trumpeting sound.

Super senses

Dinosaur fossils carry clues about how the living animals sensed the world around them – to help them find food, escape from danger, and communicate.

Fossil skin from the back has larger scales.

Scaly skin

Fossil impressions of *Triceratops* skin show a pattern of big scales, perhaps with colour – just like the colourful lizards and snakes of today.

Fossil frill skin has small scales.

Nasal cavities are behind the nostrils.

Smelling food

Big nasal cavities inside the nostrils probably gave dinosaurs a good sense of smell – useful for finding food, such as when *T rex* hunted its prey.

Colourful crests

Feathered dinosaurs might have used their plumes to show off. Fossils of *Anchiornis*, a prehistoric bird, show impressions of a colourful, feathery head crest.

Making a family

Dinosaurs probably grew fast, but like other animals they had to be old enough to have babies. When the time was right, they found a mate before laying eggs that hatched into babies.

COLOURFUL CREATURES?

Colourful birds, such as this Wilson's Bird-of-Paradise, evolved from dinosaur ancestors. Fossils show that some of these dinosaurs might have had coloured feathers or skin too – perhaps as a way of attracting mates.

Male *Nasutoceratops* lock horns in battle, perhaps over a female.

Fighting rivals

Display and combat probably helped dinosaurs get a mate. Horned dinosaurs with the biggest frills were the most impressive – especially when fighting rivals.

Male or female?

Working out the sex of a dinosaur fossil is difficult, but some scientists think that males were bigger than females as in the case of many reptiles today.

T rex females had special calcium-rich bones to help make shelled eggs.

T rex pair

Most dinosaurs were warm-blooded, like mammals today.

Diplodocus and its babies

Raising the young

Although some dinosaurs made good parents, others didn't! Their babies had to take care of themselves – especially when giant parents could accidentally crush them.

Fast facts

Yearly growth rings in fossil bones show that dinosaurs grew fast. The biggest ones probably took just a few decades to become adult.

Some dinosaurs may have danced to attract a mate like some bird species today.

Dinosaurs could breed fast too. Their numbers could recover quickly after natural disasters.

Laying eggs

Egg shells can get fossilized, in the same way as hard skeletons. When lots of fossil eggs are found together, it suggests they were laid in a nest.

Apatosaurus nests on the ground may have held clusters of 20–30 eggs.

Maiasaura families nested close together, like a seabird colony.

Nests and nurseries

Like all birds and most reptiles of today, most dinosaurs laid hard-shelled eggs. Some fossils show their eggs were laid in nests and even that the parents might have cared for their babies after hatching.

Doting parents

Maiasaura was a type of duck-billed dinosaur called a hadrosaur. Palaeontologists think it cared for its newly hatched babies.

Maiasaura packed the nest with leaves and plant parts that probably warmed the eggs and babies.

Taking off

One group of dinosaurs, called theropods, walked upright on two legs. They included giant meat-eaters, such as *T rex*, but also smaller dinosaurs that evolved wings from their arms to become birds.

Fast facts

The first flying dinosaurs may have used their wings for gliding.

Long tail feathers instead of a bony tail are better for controlling movement in the air, making birds skilful fliers.

Some prehistoric birds became flightless again – just like flightless birds of today.

Dinosaurs to birds

Fossils show that some two-legged dinosaurs grew feathers before they took to the air. Then feathers on the hands and arms grew longer and stiffer to make the flapping wings of birds.

Archaeopteryx

Velociraptor

This turkey-sized theropod had feathery arms, perhaps for keeping its balance when running.

Unlike birds of today, this early flying dinosaur had teeth in its beak, claws on its wings, and a bony tail.

First flight

No one knows exactly how the dinosaurs first took flight, but there are two possibilities: either running dinosaurs rose from the ground or climbing dinosaurs jumped out from perches.

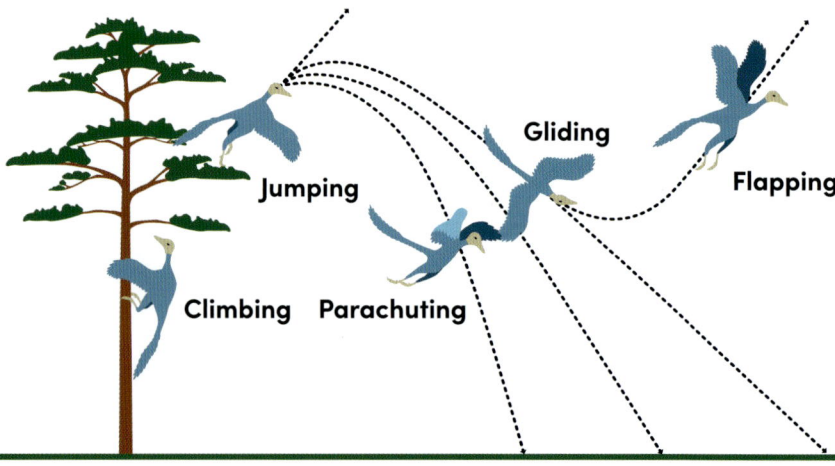

Gliding

Flapping

Jumping

Climbing   Parachuting

Running

Climbing

The pair of streaming tail feathers would break off easily if *Confuciusornis* was attacked by a predator.

Confuciusornis had up to three claws on each wing.

Short, broad wings probably helped *Iberomesornis* turn quickly in flight.

Blue-and-yellow macaw

Modern birds have a toothless beak, a feathery tail, and wings without claws.

Confuciusornis

Iberomesornis

This crow-sized bird had a toothless beak and a bony stump at the base of a long, feathery tail.

Iberomesornis was slightly bigger than a sparrow. It had good grasping toes that helped it perch on branches.

Fossil of *Anchiornis*

Anchiornis wing

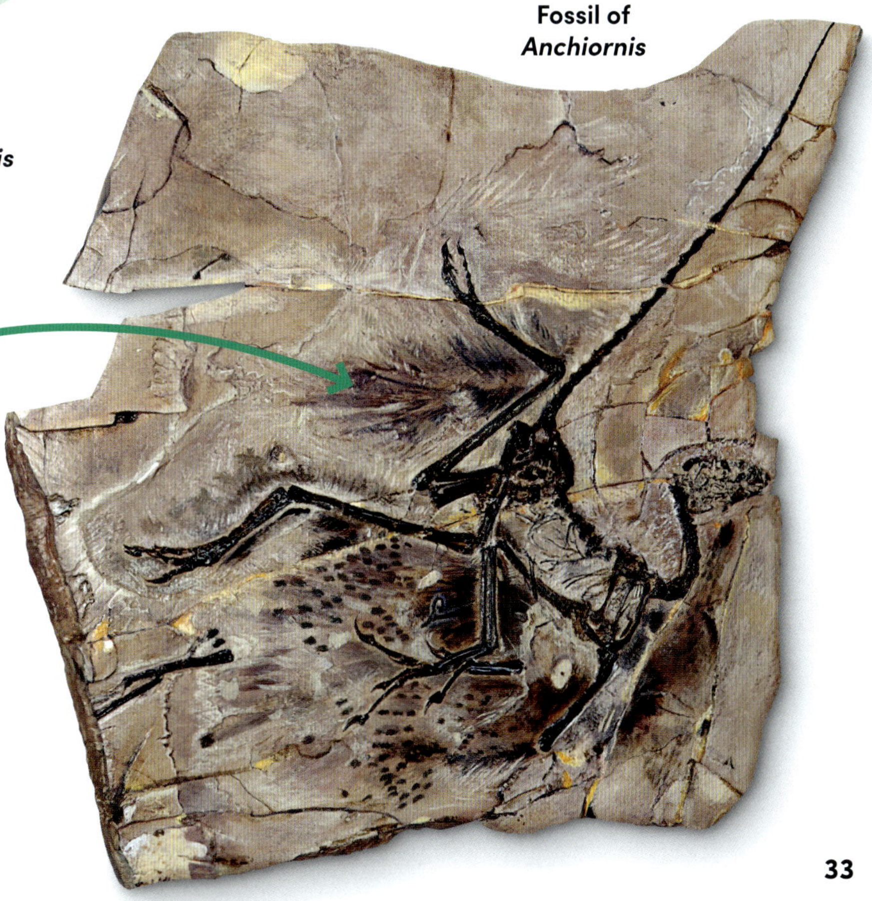

How we know

Some kinds of fossils show very good detail – including impressions of feathers big enough to be used to catch the air in flight.

Inside a dinosaur

Soft organs rot away quickly in dead animals, so they do not fossilize as well as bones and teeth. But scientists still have plenty of clues about how dinosaur bodies worked.

Plant food

Plant-eating dinosaurs probably had bigger, more complex, digestive systems than meat-eaters. Plants are tough and take longer to digest than tender meat.

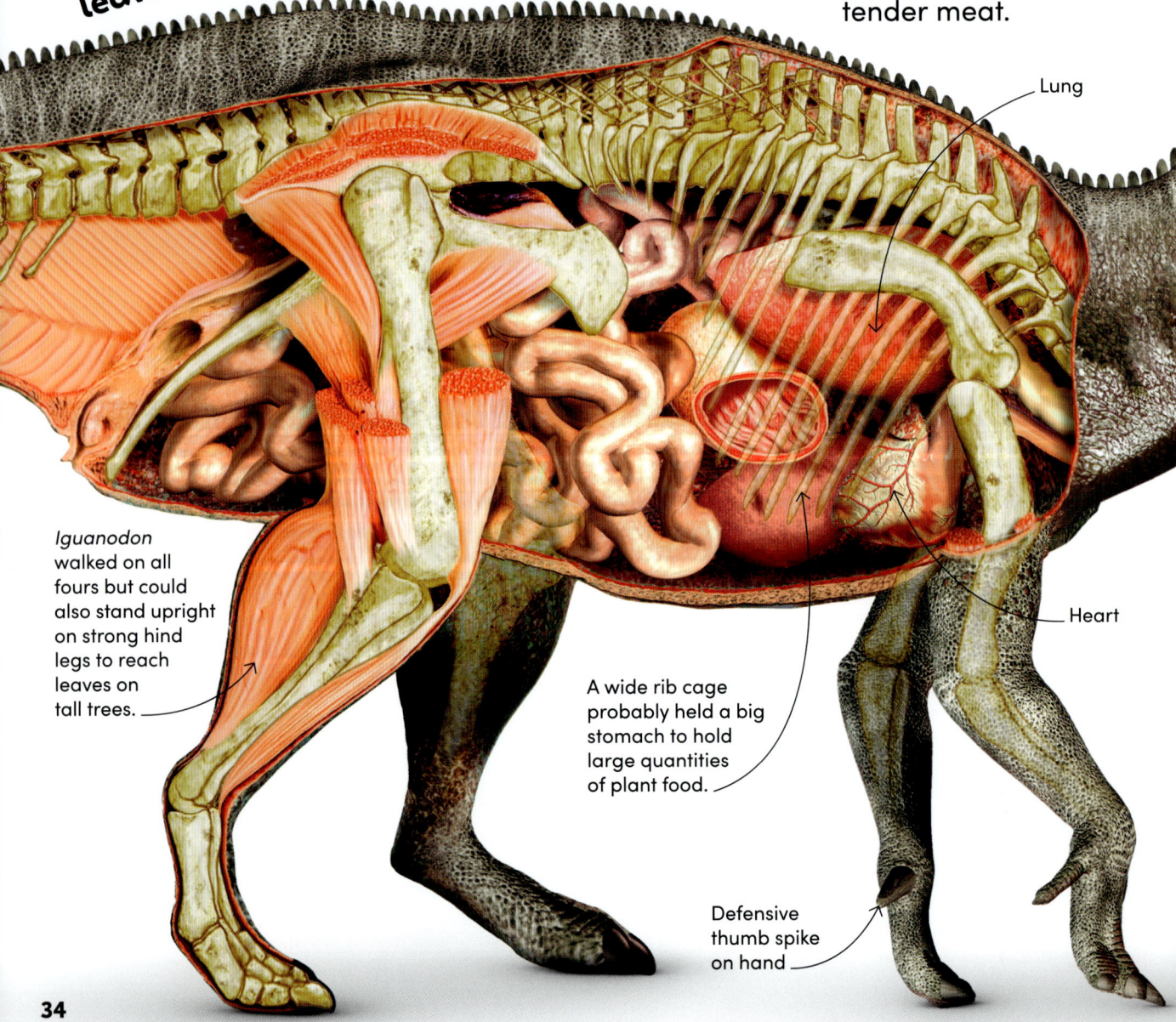

Iguanodon's teeth were ridged for grinding leaves, just like a modern iguana lizard.

Lung

Iguanodon walked on all fours but could also stand upright on strong hind legs to reach leaves on tall trees.

A wide rib cage probably held a big stomach to hold large quantities of plant food.

Heart

Defensive thumb spike on hand

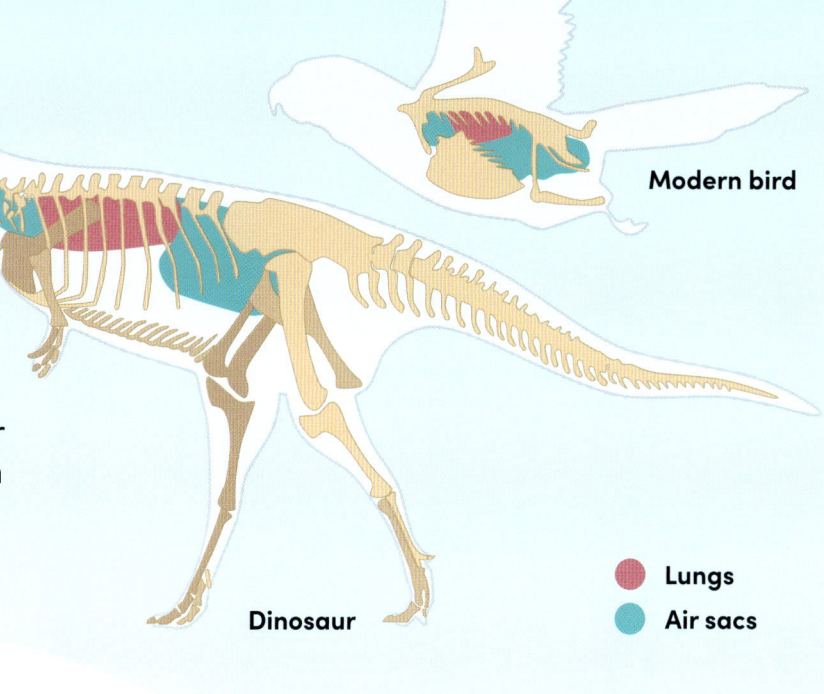

Modern bird

Air power
Just like today's birds, some dinosaurs had air spaces in their bones. This might mean that these dinosaurs breathed in a similar way, using a connected system of air sacs to flush air into and out of their lungs.

Dinosaur

● Lungs
● Air sacs

Iguanodon had cheek skin to hold food in its mouth for long periods, unlike meat-eaters.

Dino poo
Coprolites (fossilized lumps of poo) from meat-eating dinosaurs contain fragments of undigested bone, suggesting that food passed through their short gut quickly.

Grinding stones
Sometimes polished stones have been found in fossils of plant-eating dinosaurs. They were probably swallowed to help grind up tough plants.

👁 POWERFUL HEART

No one has found a fossilized dinosaur heart. But crocodiles and birds – the closest living dinosaur relatives – have a strong four-chambered heart, so dinosaur hearts were probably like this too.

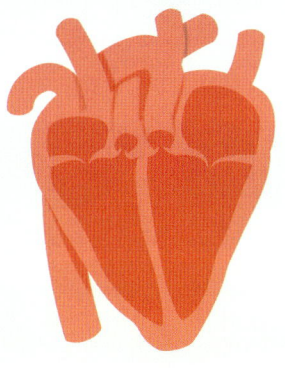

First flight

The first animals with backbones to take flight were pterosaurs. These flying reptiles had wings made of skin that stretched between their arms and legs.

Tapejara

Dinosaur neighbours

Dinosaurs didn't live alone! They shared the planet with many other types of large animals. Some of these were similar to animals we see today, but others were in a group of their own.

Fast facts

Big prehistoric crocodiles and even some mammals probably hunted the smallest dinosaurs.

The biggest pterosaur, *Quetzalcoatlus*, had a wingspan three times that of today's largest albatross.

Pterosaurs and giant marine reptiles went extinct, with most dinosaurs, 66 million years ago.

Crocodile ancestors

Some prehistoric ancestors of today's crocodile grew into giants, and a few even walked on two legs, just like some dinosaurs.

Kaprosuchus

Early mammals

The first hairy mammals were small and ate insects. They probably moved around at night to stay safe from the bigger meat-eating dinosaurs that hunted during the day.

Megazostrodon was a tiny, shrew-like mammal.

Marine giants

The seas and oceans were home to many reptiles such as the short-necked *Liopleurodon* and the long-necked *Plesiosaurus*.

Liopluerodon had four strong, paddle-like limbs that made it a swift swimmer.

End of the dinosaurs

About 66 million years ago, our planet suffered a catastrophe that was so big it wiped out many creatures on Earth. This mass extinction ended the reign of the dinosaurs.

The asteriod hit Earth with the force of 20 million nuclear bombs.

Danger!
A space rock, called an asteroid, struck Earth with immense power. It created earthquakes, tsunamis, and wildfires, and filled the air with dust.

Super volcanoes

In India, massive volcanoes, called the Deccan Traps, were erupting when the asteroid hit – making the global disaster even worse.

Climate change

At first dust in the sky blocked the Sun and chilled the planet for years. But then carbon dioxide from shattered rock baked Earth like a giant oven.

Didelphodon had a long otter-like body.

Survivors

Small, warm-blooded mammals, such as *Didelphodon*, probably survived by burrowing underground. They were the ancestors of mammals alive today.

 LIVING DINOSAURS

In a sense, dinosaurs were not completely wiped out. The birds that evolved from upright meat-eating theropods survived. They continued the dinosaur line in feathery form, developing into the wide range of birds we see today. One large prehistoric bird was *Gastornis.* This flightless creature lived in North America and Europe.

All about fossils

Dinosaurs have left their mark in the ground, even though they lived and died hundreds of millions of years ago. This is because their bodies and footprints have turned into rocky fossils.

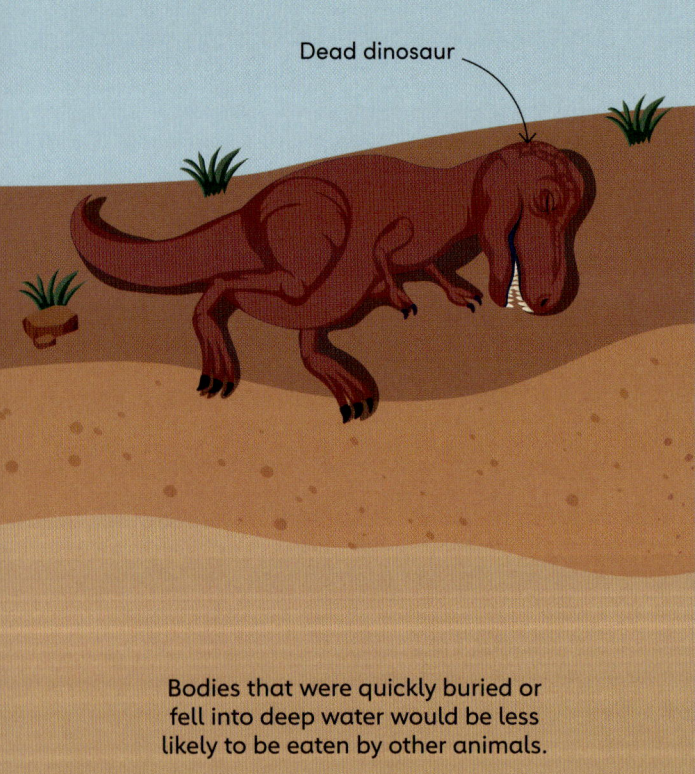

Dead dinosaur

Particles called sediment surrounded the body and stuck together to make layers of sedimentary rock.

Bodies that were quickly buried or fell into deep water would be less likely to be eaten by other animals.

Heavy soil squeezed water out of the buried body, slowing the decay of soft flesh and gradually revealing the hard skeleton.

Dino fossils

Fossils can be any trace of life from millions of years ago. As well as solid bones, footprints, and other impressions, they include tiny animals in amber and even lumps of rocky poo!

Skull bones of
Styracosaurus

Dinosaur feather in amber (hardened tree resin)

Making a fossil

Over millions of years, minerals seep into the body of a dead dinosaur and turn it into rock, until land movements bring it closer to the surface.

Fast facts

The hardest body parts, such as teeth and bones, are more likely to survive as fossils.

Dinosaurs that were suddenly buried under landslides or volcanic eruptions have left the best complete fossils.

Scientists can work out how long fossils have been in the ground by doing chemical tests on the rocks around them.

New lake formed

Water that seeped into bones drained away, leaving minerals in place, which turned the skeleton into rock.

Palaeontologist

Land movements pushed the rock upwards, while wind and rain wore away the surface to expose the dino fossil.

Skin impression of *Barosaurus*

Dinosaur skull mould

Coprolite (fossil poo) of *Titanosaurus*

Digging up dinosaurs

Scientists called palaeontologists study prehistoric life and fossils. They dig up dinosaur fossils in old rocks – from the Triassic, Jurassic, and Cretaceous periods.

Buried bones

Digging in the right place relies on luck and judgement. Sometimes bits of skeleton are sticking out of the rock's surface, and small bone fragments can mean a bigger fossil lies underneath.

Plaster protection

Fossils break easily, so a plaster cast is made around the fossil to protect it before moving it to a museum.

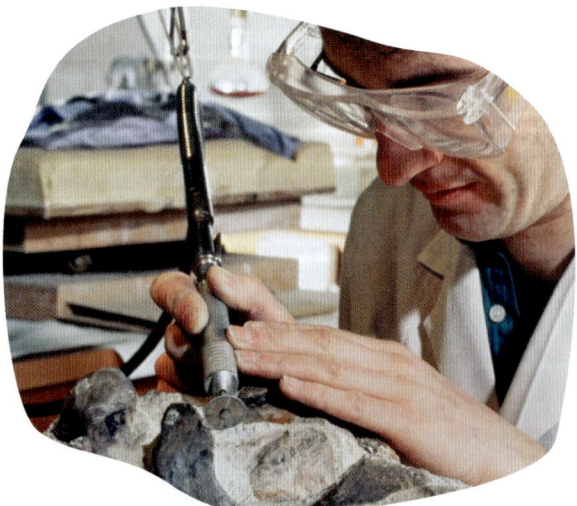

Careful cleaning

In the museum's lab, the cast is removed and the rest of the rock and dust is cleared away from the fossil. Broken bones are fixed with glue.

Jigsaw puzzle

Bones can move before they form
fossils in the ground, and some might
be lost altogether. Surviving bones are
put together to make a skeleton.

Dinosaur dig site
in Alberta, Canada

Building dinosaurs

Modern technology means that today's scientists can make images and models of dinosaurs that are more realistic than ever before. Much of this starts with work on fossil skeletons.

Fossil display

Dinosaur bones are studied and compared with skeletons of animals alive today. This helps scientists build skeletons that are standing in the right position to match the most likely posture of the living dinosaur.

Some dinosaur skeletons on display are artificial replicas.

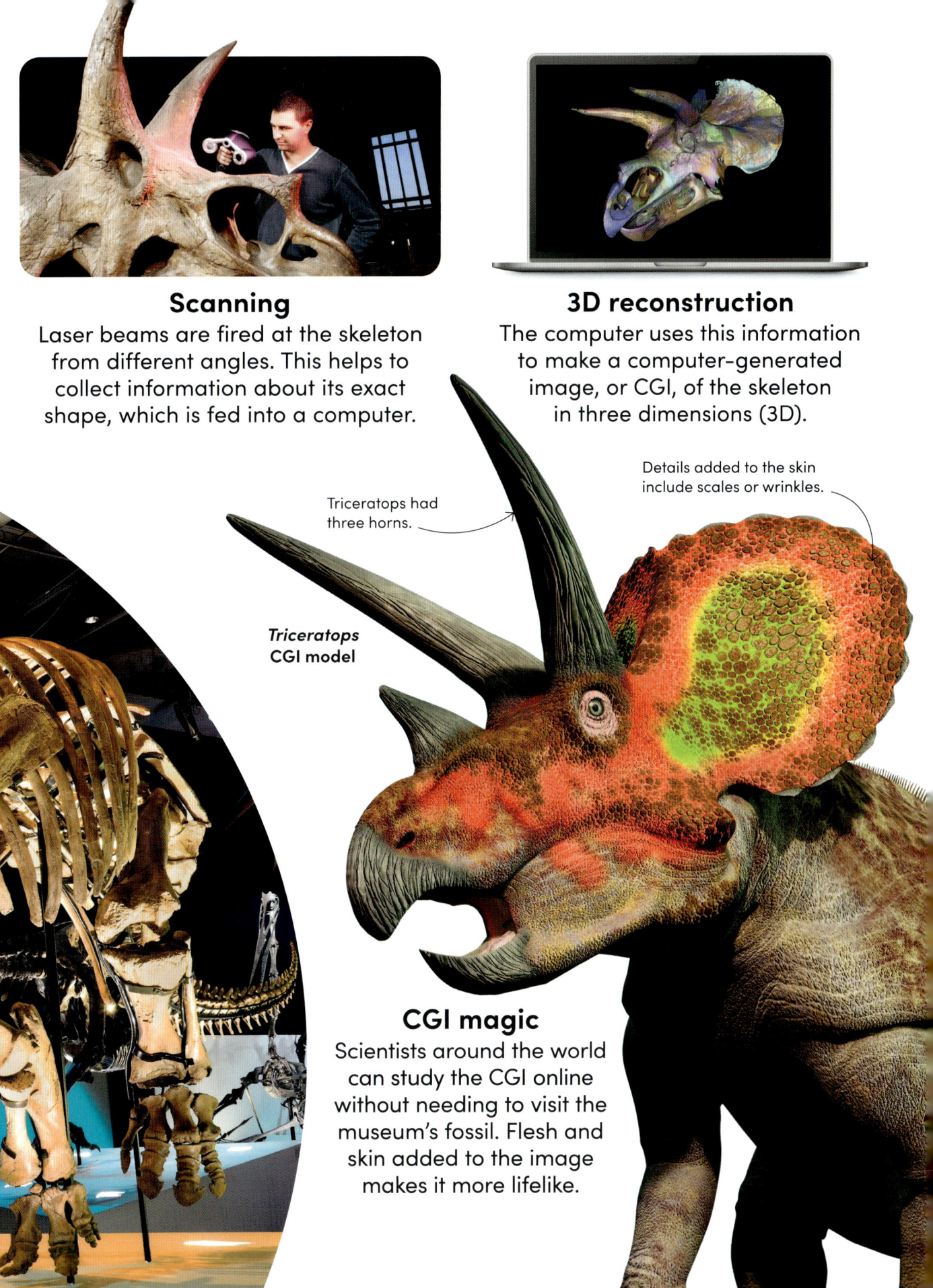

Scanning

Laser beams are fired at the skeleton from different angles. This helps to collect information about its exact shape, which is fed into a computer.

3D reconstruction

The computer uses this information to make a computer-generated image, or CGI, of the skeleton in three dimensions (3D).

Triceratops had three horns.

Details added to the skin include scales or wrinkles.

Triceratops
CGI model

CGI magic

Scientists around the world can study the CGI online without needing to visit the museum's fossil. Flesh and skin added to the image makes it more lifelike.

Facts match

How much do you know about dinosaurs? Read the clues and see if you can find the correct answers among the pictures.

2
This **long-necked giant** was **flat-footed.**

1
This tiny flier was one of the first dinosaurs to **take to the air**.

Velociraptor

Struthiomimus

Archaeopteryx fossil

T rex

Nasutoceratops

Herrerasaurus

Kentrosaurus

8
The fossil of this bird-like dinosaur shows that it had **flight feathers and hollow bones**.

7
With **sharp spikes all over its tail**, this dinosaur was more than a match for any predator.

9
This dinosaur might have used its **thick, bony skull** to headbutt its rivals.

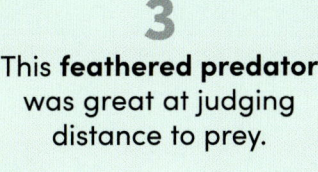

3
This **feathered predator** was great at judging distance to prey.

5
From its skull, you can tell that this dinosaur's mouth was shaped **like a duck's bill** and had hundreds of tiny teeth.

4
Just like a crocodile, this dinosaur had protective **bony plates called scutes** in its skin.

6
This dinosaur **walked on its tippy toes**.

Hypacrosaurus skull

Stegouros

Argentinosaurus

Pachycephalosaurus

Microraptor

12
This predator had a **powerful, bone-crushing bite**.

11
Locking horns with rivals in a duel might have helped this dinosaur **win a mate**.

10
This was an **early meat-eating dinosaur**.

Where are my eggs?

Help the *Orodromeus* reach her eggs by answering the questions correctly and revealing the path she must take through the forest.

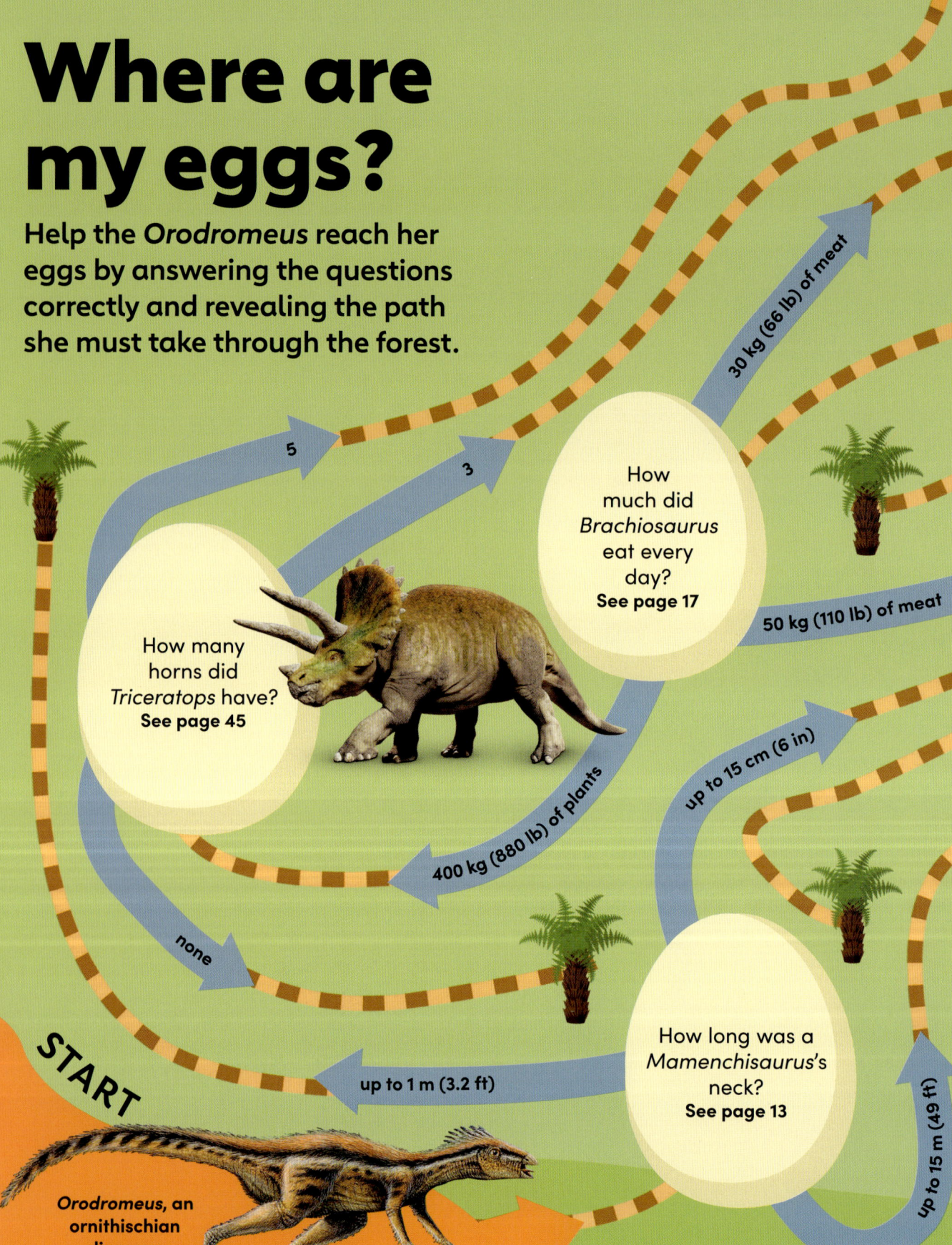

5

3

30 kg (66 lb) of meat

How much did *Brachiosaurus* eat every day?
See page 17

50 kg (110 lb) of meat

How many horns did *Triceratops* have?
See page 45

up to 15 cm (6 in)

400 kg (880 lb) of plants

up to 1 m (3.2 ft)

How long was a *Mamenchisaurus*'s neck?
See page 13

up to 15 m (49 ft)

START

Orodromeus, an ornithischian dinosaur

Ankylosaurus could ward off attackers by using its...
See page 25

bony crest

clubbed tail

Brachiosaurus

bony sail

Which dinosaur had teeth shaped like pencils?
See page 16

on its tippy toes

on its flat feet

Diplodocus

T rex

How did *Struthiomimus* walk?
See page 14

it flew everywhere

FINISH

Dig that bone

Can you match the correct skeleton to the correct dinosaur? Read the clues to the bone fragments and find out their rightful owners.

1
Sharp claws on each foot made this small meat-eater a deadly hunter.

2
A long neck made it easy for this plant-eater to reach leaves on treetops.

5
Attackers would be wary of the heavy, clubbed tail of this plant-eater.

6
The largest predator of all time had a massive sail on its back.

Triceratops

Stegosaurus

Velociraptor

Ankylosaurus

Spinosaurus

Archaeopteryx

Brachiosaurus

Parasaurolophus

3

This dinosaur had prominent head horns, probably used when it charged at rivals.

4

A toothed beak and clawed wings were features of this early flying dinosaur.

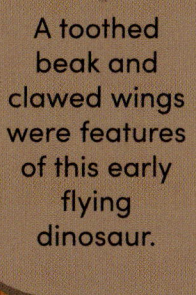

7

This dinosaur's hollow horn might have made a trumpeting sound like an elephant.

8

A double line of bony plates on its back made this dinosaur easy to identify.

Answers: 1.Velociraptor 2.Brachiosaurus 3.Triceratops 4.Archaeopteryx 5.Ankylosaurus 6.Spinosaurus 7.Parasaurolophus 8.Stegosaurus

Dinosaur danger

You have been transported to a world filled with dinosaurs and other prehistoric creatures. Can you race past them to reach home safely?

You're home!

Cretaceous

Skirt past the Ankylosaurus's clubbed tail. **Move two spaces.**

A Nasutoceratops is charging at you with its horned head on display. Hide. **Miss a turn.**

That's a deadly *Allosaurus*. Climb up a tree and hide. **Miss a turn.**

Wait, don't cross the river. Is that a *Smilosuchus* lurking there? Wait for it to slink away. **Miss a turn.**

That's a *Postosuchus* coming towards you with its deadly teeth bared. Run for your life. **Move two spaces.**

Triassic

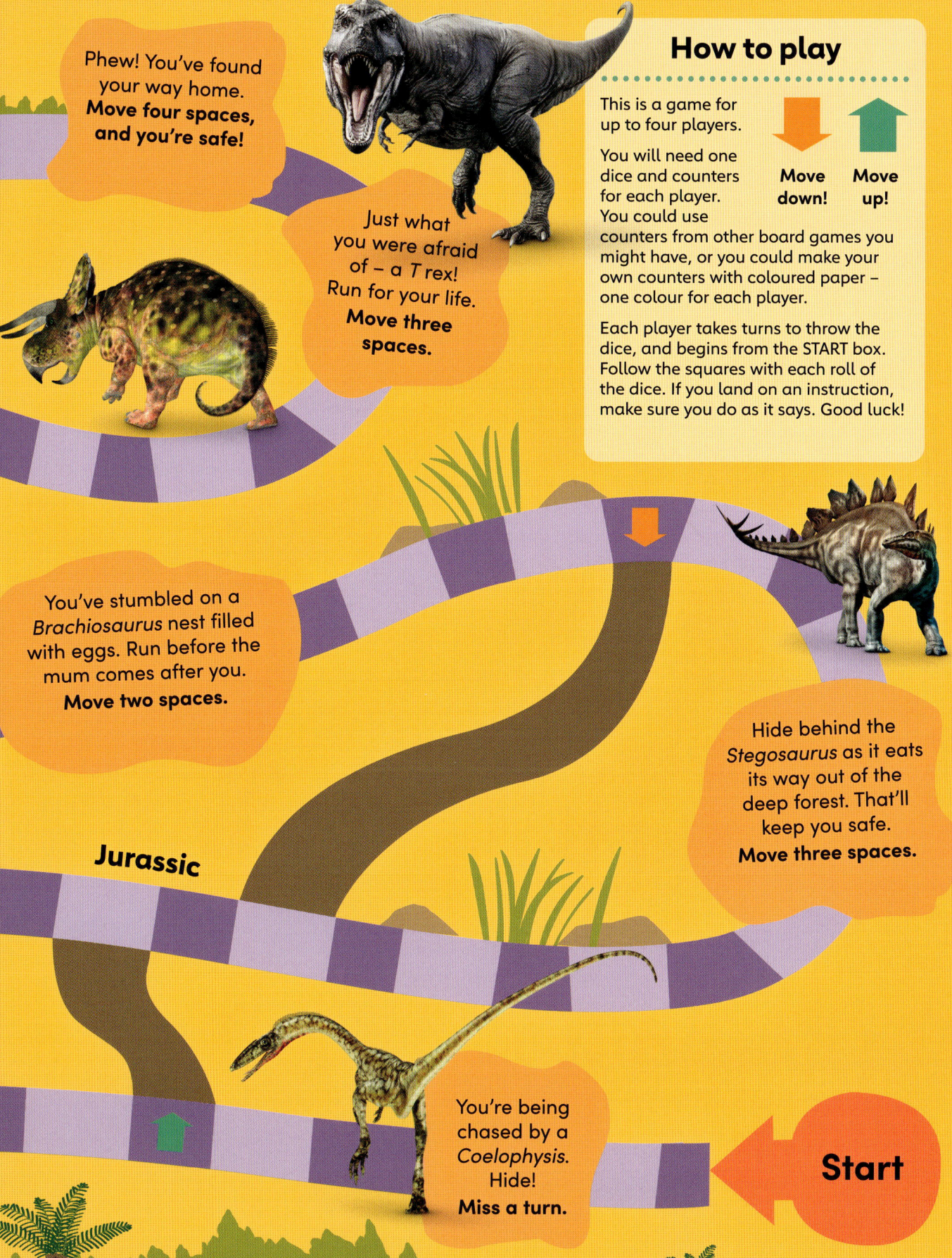

Phew! You've found your way home. **Move four spaces, and you're safe!**

Just what you were afraid of – a *T* rex! Run for your life. **Move three spaces.**

How to play

This is a game for up to four players.

Move down!

Move up!

You will need one dice and counters for each player. You could use counters from other board games you might have, or you could make your own counters with coloured paper – one colour for each player.

Each player takes turns to throw the dice, and begins from the START box. Follow the squares with each roll of the dice. If you land on an instruction, make sure you do as it says. Good luck!

You've stumbled on a *Brachiosaurus* nest filled with eggs. Run before the mum comes after you. **Move two spaces.**

Hide behind the *Stegosaurus* as it eats its way out of the deep forest. That'll keep you safe. **Move three spaces.**

Jurassic

You're being chased by a *Coelophysis*. Hide! **Miss a turn.**

Start

Glossary

Air sacs Balloon-like, air-filled compartments in the body that help supply air to lungs.

Amber Hardened fossil resin from prehistoric trees.

Asteroid A lump of space rock that orbits the Sun.

Breeding When living things produce eggs or babies to increase their numbers.

Brooding The way an animal, especially a bird, sits on eggs or young to protect them and keep them warm. Egg-laying dinosaurs also might have brooded over their clutch of eggs.

Conifer An evergreen tree that produces seeds in cones.

Continent One of Earth's great land masses.

Coprolite Fossilized dinosaur poo found by palaeontologists.

Crest A cluster of feathers, or a bony projection on the head, probably for display.

Cretaceous The last period of the dinosaur age. It began around 145 million years ago and ended 66 million years ago.

Dinosaurs Prehistoric reptiles with upright limbs that dominated life on land in the Triassic, Jurassic, and Cretaceous periods.

Duck-billed A mouth shaped like a duck's pointy bill.

Extinction The death of a species.

Fossil The preserved remains of a long-dead animal or plant.

Frill A bony projection around the head or neck.

Ginkgo One of the oldest known tree species in the world. It is commonly known as the maidenhair tree.

Ichthyosaur A group of aquatic reptiles from prehistoric times that are now extinct.

Jurassic The middle period of the dinosaur age. It began about 201 million years ago and ended about 145 million years ago.

Mammal A warm-blooded animal with a hairy body. Female mammals produce milk to feed their young babies.

Palaeontologist A scientist who studies prehistoric life, including fossils. Many palaeontologists concentrate on studying dinosaurs.

Predator An animal that hunts another animal for food.

Prehistoric Belonging to a time before history was recorded by humans in written form.

Prey An animal that is hunted by another animal for food.

Pterosaur Prehistoric flying reptiles that evolved during the Triassic Period, and lived alongside dinosaurs.

Reptile A cold-blooded, air-breathing animal covered in hard scales.

Sauropod A large, plant-eating dinosaur, typically with a small head, and a long neck and tail.

Scales Small, thin plates that protect the skin of reptiles and fish.

Scavenge To eat the dead remains of an animal.

Scutes Protective bony plates in the skin, as seen in crocodiles and turtles.

Species A group of creatures made up of related individuals who are able to produce young with one another.

Theropod A two-legged, meat-eating dinosaur. Some theropods were the ancestors of modern birds.

Triassic The first part of the dinosaur age. It lasted from about 252 to 201 million years ago. Dinosaurs evolved towards the end of the Triassic Period.

Warm-blooded Animals that can keep their body temperature the same, even when the temperature around them changes. Mammals and birds are warm-blooded, and dinosaurs may have been warm-blooded, too.

Animal alphabet

Prehistoric animals mentioned in this book that lived in the Triassic, Jurassic, and Cretaceous periods are listed here in alphabetical order. Use the page numbers to find them.

Allosaurus 22, 23, 52
Pronunciation: ah-loh-SOR-us
Period: Jurassic

Anchiornis 27, 33
Pronunciation: AHNG-kee-OR-nis
Period: Jurassic

Ankylosaurus 9, 25, 49, 51
Pronunciation: an-KYE-lo-SOR-us
Period: Cretaceous

Apatosaurus 30
Pronunciation: uh-PAT-uh-SOR-uhs
Period: Jurassic

Archaeopteryx 7, 15, 32, 47, 51
Pronunciation: ark-ee-OPT-er-iks
Period: Jurassic

Argentinosaurus 8, 15, 47
Pronunciation: Ar-jen-TEEN-oh-SOR-us
Period: Cretaceous

Austroraptor 20
Pronunciation: AUS-tro-RAP-tor
Period: Cretaceous

Barosaurus 41
Pronunciation: BAHR-uh-SOR-uhs
Period: Jurassic

Brachiosaurus 17, 48, 51, 53
Pronunciation: BRACK-io-SOR-us
Period: Jurassic

Carnotaurus 4
Pronunciation: car-noh-TOR-us
Period: Cretaceous

Coelophysis 11
Pronunciation: see-low-FIE-sis
Period: Triassic

Confuciusornis 33
Pronunciation: con-FYOO-shuhs-OR-nis
Period: Cretaceous

Didelphodon 39
Pronunciation: die-DELL-foe-don
Period: Cretaceous

Diplodocus 6, 7, 16, 22, 29
Pronunciation: DIP-LOW-doh-cuss
Period: Jurassic

Edmontonia 16
Pronunciation: ed-mon-TOE-nee-a
Period: Cretaceous

Einiosaurus 25
Pronunciation: EYE-ni-uh-SOR-us
Period: Cretaceous

Herrerasaurus 8, 18, 46
Pronunciation: Her-REER-row-SOR-us
Period: Triassic

Heterodontosaurus 9
Pronunciation: HET-uh-roh-DON-toh-SOR-us
Period: Jurassic

Hypacrosaurus 17, 47
Pronunciation: Hi-PACK-crow-SOR-us
Period: Cretaceous

Iberomesornis 33
Pronunciation: I-ber-o-MES-OR-nis
Period: Cretaceous

Iguanodon 9, 34, 35
Pronunciation: ih-GWAH-nuh-don
Period: Cretaceous

Kaprosuchus 36
Pronunciation: KAP-roh-SUE-kus
Period: Cretaceous

Kentrosaurus 25, 47
Pronunciation: KEN-tro-SOR-us
Period: Jurassic

Liopleurodon 37
Pronunciation: le-oh-PLUR-oh-don
Period: Jurassic

Maiasaura 30, 31
Pronunciation: mie-uh-SOR-ruh
Period: Cretaceous

Mamenchisaurus 12, 13
Pronunciation: ma-MAN-chee-SOR-us
Period: Jurassic

Megazostrodon 37
Pronunciation: mega-ZOS-tro-don
Period: Triassic

Microraptor 12, 13, 47
Pronunciation: MI-cro-RAP-tur
Period: Cretaceous

Nasutoceratops 28, 46, 52
Pronunciation: NAH-soo-toe-SER-uh-tops
Period: Cretaceous

Oviraptor 30
Pronunciation: OH-vee-RAP-tor
Period: Cretaceous

Pachycephalosaurus 9, 25, 47
Pronunciation: pah-kee-sef-uh-loh-SOR-us
Period: Cretaceous

Parasaurolophus 26, 51
Pronunciation: par-uh-SAWR-uh-LOH-fus
Period: Cretaceous

Plesiosaurus 37
Pronunciation: PLEASE-ee-oh-SOR-us
Period: Jurassic

Postosuchus 52
Pronunciation: POST-oh-SOO-kus
Period: Triassic

Psittacosaurus 24
Pronunciation: sih-TACK-oh-sor-us
Period: Cretaceous

Quetzalcoatlus 36
Pronunciation: ket-suhl-koh-AT-luhss
Period: Cretaceous

Quilmesaurus 24
Pronunciation: QUILL-meh-SOR-us
Period: Cretaceous

Saltasaurus 24
Pronunciation: sal-tuh-SOR-us
Period: Cretaceous

Smilosuchus 52
Pronunciation: S-my-loh-SOO-kus
Period: Triassic

Spinosaurus 18, 22, 51
Pronunciation: Spy-no-SOR-us
Period: Cretaceous

Stegosaurus 6, 9, 23, 51, 53
Pronunciation: steg-oh-SOR-us
Period: Jurassic

Stegouros 25, 47
Pronunciation: STEG-uh-rus
Period: Cretaceous

Struthiomimus 14, 46, 49
Pronunciation: stroo-thee-oh-MIGH-muhs
Period: Cretaceous

Styracosaurus 40
Pronunciation: sty-RACK-oh-SOR-us
Period: Cretaceous

Tapejara 36
Pronunciation: tap-uh-JAH-ruh
Period: Cretaceous

Titanosaurus 41
Pronunciation: tie-TAN-oh-SOR-us
Period: Cretaceous

Triceratops 9, 19, 21, 27, 45, 48, 51
Pronunciation: try-SER-a-tops
Period: Cretaceous

Tyrannosaurus rex 8, 11, 19, 21, 23, 27, 29, 46, 53
Pronunciation: Tie-RAN-oh-SOR-us REX
Period: Cretaceous

Velociraptor 23, 26, 32, 46, 51
Pronunciation: veh-LO-si-RAP-tor
Period: Cretaceous

Yangchuanosaurus 13
Pronunciation: YANG-choo-AHN-o-SOR-us
Period: Jurassic

Index

AB
air sacs 35
amber 40
ankylosaurs 9
armour 6, 25
asteroids 38–39
babies 21, 29, 31
backbones 6
birds 5, 32–33, 35, 39
bones 6–7, 35,
    42–43
bony plates 6, 25
breeding 28–29
brooding 30

CD
ceratopsians 7, 9
claws 18, 22, 32–33
climate change 39
computer technology 45
continents 11
coprolites 41
Cretaceous Period
    10–11

crocodiles 4, 36
Deccan Traps 39
defences 24–25
digestive system 34
duck-bills 17

EF
eggs 30–31
extinction 38–39
feathers 7, 32–33
feet 15, 22
females 29
fish 18
flight 7, 32–33, 36
footprints 21, 40
fossils 33, 40–41,
    42, 44
frills 25, 28

GH
Gastornis 39
grazing 16
hadrosaurs 31
heart 35
herds 20–21, 25
hips 4, 8–9
horns 25, 28

IJL
ichthyosaurs 5
jaws 19, 22
Jurassic Period 10–11
legs 4, 7, 14–15
lizards 4, 8
lungs 35

MNO
males 29
mammals 11, 37, 39
marine animals 5, 37
mass extinction 38–39
mating displays 28
meat-eaters 18–19,
    22–23, 35
museums 42, 44–45
neck 13, 16
nests 30–31
organs 34–35
ornithopods 9

PS
pachycephalosaurs 7, 9
packs 22
palaeontology 42–43
Pangaea 11

pelvis 8
plant-eaters 9, 16–17, 24, 34
plates 6, 25
poo 35, 41
predators 18–19, 22–23, 25
prey 22–23
protection 24–25
pterosaurs 5, 36
sauropods 8, 11, 12, 15
scales 4
scavengers 20
scutes 25
skeletons 7, 44–45
skull 19, 22
stegosaurs 9

TVW
tail 5, 7, 25
technology 44–45
teeth 16–17, 18–19, 22, 34
theropods 8, 18, 22–23, 32
toes 14–15
Triassic Period 10–11
volcanoes 39
wings 13, 15, 32–33, 36

Acknowledgments

The publisher would like to thank the following people for their help with making the book: Upamanyu Das, Shahid Qureshi, and Zarak Rais for editorial assistance; Revati Anand and Heena Sharma for design assistance; Anita Yadav for pre-production design assistance; Samrajkumar S for picture credits; Caroline Stamps for proofreading; and Elizabeth Wise for indexing.

The publisher would like to thank the following for their kind permission to reproduce their photographs:

(Key: a-above; b-below/bottom; c-centre; f-far; l-left; r-right; t-top)

123RF.com: Linda Bucklin 5bc, Leonello Calvetti 9tr, Mark Turner 47cb; **Adobe Stock:** Dottedyeti 9br, 48c; **Alamy Stock Photo:** All Canada Photos / Roderick Chen 42–43, Leonello Calvetti 27cr, 53bc, Corbin17 27tr, 44–45, Daniel Eskridge 3br, 16–17, Don Geyer 16c (Background), Mohamad Haghani 3tl, 14br, 25bl, 36t, 46ca, Christian Kitzmüller 30c, Minden Pictures / Mike Parry 22br, Minden Pictures / Otto Plantema / Buiten-beeld 28cra, Natural Visions / Heather Angel 38–39tc, NPS 52bc, Prawns 35cr, Lee Rentz 41bl, Science Photo Library / Leonello Calvetti 25cr, 52cla, Science Photo Library / Mark Garlick 38–39b, Science Photo Library / Roger Harris 22bc, Science Photo Library / Sebastian Kaulitzki 25br, Martin Shields 33br, Witold Skrypczak 6–7, Stocktrek Images, Inc. / Mark Hallett 20–21, Stocktrek Images, Inc. / Mohamad Haghani 25tr, 30tl, 47c, Stocktrek Images, Inc. / Nobumichi Tamura 39cl, Stocktrek Images, Inc. / Phil Wilson 48bl, Stocktrek Images, Inc. / Walter Myers 45br, The Natural History Museum 35clb, 41br, Jim West 21cra, Gary Whitton 41bc; **Davide Bonadonna:** Davide Bonadonna 18–19t; **Depositphotos Inc:** Blueringmedia 40–41, KostPhoto 13cb, Pixelchaos 50bl; **Dorling Kindersley:** American Museum of Natural History / Lynton Gardiner 3tr, 17tc, 47cla, Chatterjee, Sankar & Templin, R. (2012). Earth and Life. 10.1007 / 978-90-481-3428-1_18 32b, Colorado Plateau Geosystems Inc. / Simon Mumford 11tr, 11cra, 11crb, Dan Crisp 48–49 (Cycad Plant), Jon Hughes 9tl, James Kuether 8tl, 9bl, 24clb, Natural History Museum, London / John Downes / John Holmes - Modelmaker 49br, Senckenberg Gesellschaft Fuer

Naturforschung Museum / Gary Ombler 16bl, Senckenberg Nature Museum / Andy Crawford 7cr, 46c, The Natural History Museum / Lynton Gardiner 40bl, Turbosquid: Coolnidz / Arran Lewis 33clb; **Dreamstime.com:** Alinamd 27clb (Background), Linda Bucklin 36b, 46clb, Leonello Calvetti 18bc, 46cb, 49tl, Ihor Deyneka 50cr, 51bl, Elena Duvernay 15tr, Daniel Eskridge 2br, 4–5, 9bc, 26b, 47clb, Corey A Ford 29cr, 53cla, Fabio Iozzino 22tl, Isselee 33tr, Juliengrondin 39cra, Anton Lunkov 51cr, Lina Moiseienko 16t, Mr1805 5br, William Roberts 39br, Sontaya999 16tl, Mark Turner 53tc, 53cr; **Getty Images:** Sergey Krasovskiy 13cr, Science Photo Library / Mark Garlick 52cr, Stocktrek Images / Leonello Calvetti 34–35, Sygma / Didier Dutheil 42clb; **Getty Images / iStock:** Rodrusoleg 45tr (Laptop), Seamartini 50br, 50–51 (Background), 51cl, 51br; **Júlia d'Oliveira:** Júlia d'Oliveira 12–13; **The Natural History Museum, London:** 6tc; **Science Photo Library:** Carlton Publishing Group 27br, JA Chirinos 24–25, 36–37b, Pascal Goetgheluck 40br, 45tl, James Kuether 22–23, 22cl, 28–29b, 29tr, 30–31b, 31tr, Natural History Museum, London 42crb, Jose Antonio Peñas 20tl, Philippe Psaila 43clb, Detlev Van Ravenswaay 40bc, Smithsonian Institute 45tr, Mark P. Witton 19br; **Shutterstock.com:** Happyfunnydrawings 50cl.

Cover images: Front: Adobe Stock: Sebastian Kaulitzki cl/ (*Protoceratops*), cb; **Dorling Kindersley:** Andy Crawford Courtesy of Dorset Dinosaur Museum ca/ (Egg), Peter Minister, Digital Sculptor br, Natural History Museum, London / Colin Keates cl, cra/ (Skull), cr, crb, crb/ (Foot), Natural History Museum, London / Tim Parmenter bl, Royal Tyrrell Museum of Palaeontology, Alberta, Canada / Andy Crawford cla, c/ (Skull); **Getty Images:** Stocktrek Images / Mohamad Haghani cra, bc/ (*Shunosaurus*), Stocktrek Images / Sergey Krasovskiy cra/ (*Tupandactylus*); **Getty Images / iStock:** Crazytang bc; **Science Photo Library:** Mark Garlick c, Detlev Van Ravenswaay ca; **Back: Adobe Stock:** Sebastian Kaulitzki tl; **Alamy Stock Photo:** Anjo Kan tc; **Dorling Kindersley:** James Kuether cla, bc, Natural History Museum, London / Colin Keates clb/ (Foot), Senckenberg Nature Museum / Andy Crawford clb, The Natural History Museum / Lynton Gardiner cr; **Dreamstime.com:** Elena Duvernay crb, Corey A Ford cra; **Getty Images:** Mark Garlick cl.